Back to Basics™

YEAR 5

NAPLAN*-style LANGUAGE CONVENTIONS

Do you need to go back to the basics and practise language conventions for NAPLAN? Let's read together and learn.

Parents and carers are encouraged to read the explanation and practice sections with their child.

Stella Tarakson

Illustrated by
Janice Bowles

*This is not an officially endorsed publication of the NAPLAN program and is produced by Pascal Press independently of Australian Governments.

About this book

This book is designed to review the skills required for the Language Conventions component of the year 5 NAPLAN* test and to practise NAPLAN-style questions.

The book commences with a pre-test, to help identify any areas of weakness that may require special attention.

It is then divided into three sections: spelling, grammar and punctuation. Each section is composed of eight units.

Each unit begins with a brief explanation of a particular concept. This is followed by examples of how this concept is used **(We practise)**. Practical exercises are then provided to give your child the opportunity to practise the concept **(You practise)**. These exercises reinforce the concept and check that your child understands it fully.

We recommend that your child take the eight-page pull-out test under timed conditions, once the bulk of the book has been successfully completed.

If further instruction is required, we recommend that this book be provided to your child's teacher for review. Then the parent or carer and the teacher can devise a plan to ensure all the basic contents are fully understood and consolidated.

Meet 'BOB' – Back Of the Book

At the end of each unit, BOB reminds your child to go to the Answers section at the back of the book.

*This is not an officially endorsed publication of the NAPLAN program and is produced by Pascal Press independently of Australian Governments.

Contents & Checklist

INTRODUCTION to NAPLAN*

The National Assessment Program for Literacy and Numeracy (NAPLAN) is a Federal Government initiative that requires the assessment of skills in literacy and numeracy across all Australian schools for students in years 3, 5, 7 and 9. It was introduced in 2008 to replace the previous state-based assessment programs.

NAPLAN is held annually in May. All students receive an individualised report on their performance, which can be compared to the average performance of all students in Australia. The report contains a description of each assessment area, and identifies the skills being assessed.

Using this book to prepare for the NAPLAN test

The NAPLAN Language Conventions test covers Spelling, Grammar and Punctuation and is largely based on multiple-choice questions. Students are required to identify the correct answer to a question by shading the correct bubble. Some questions, require written answers.

The units in this book are divided into three sections — spelling, grammar and punctuation — and are based on previous NAPLAN tests.

Pre-Test

A Pre-Test has been included on pages 6–7 to help you identify your child's areas of weakness. Once completed, use the marking grid on page 7 to guide you to the units that will be most helpful. Answers are supplied on page 62.

Mini-Tests

The Spelling, Grammar and Punctuation sections are each followed by two Mini-Tests. We recommend that your child take a Mini-Test every time they complete four units. Check your child's results by looking at the answers at the back of the book, and discuss any incorrect ones with them.

Pull-out test

This book comes with an eight-page removable Sample NAPLAN test. This will give your child a good idea of what to expect during the actual exam. The results will provide the information you need to pinpoint areas that require attention. We recommend that your child take this test under timed conditions when the bulk of the book has been successfully completed.

*This is not an officially endorsed publication of the NAPLAN program and is produced by Pascal Press independently of Australian Governments.

HINTS and TIPS

Exam equipment:

- ✳ Make sure you have at least TWO sharp HB or 2B pencils—in case one breaks.
- ✳ Make sure you have an eraser—in case you mark the wrong bubble by mistake.

Reading time:

- ✳ Read all the instructions carefully.
- ✳ Read each question TWICE so you understand exactly what is being asked.

Answering multiple-choice questions:

- ✳ First, try to answer the question without looking at the choices. Once you think you know the correct answer, read through the choices.
- ✳ Fill in the answer bubble properly

like this  

NOT like this  ✗

Timing:

- ✳ You will have 40 minutes to do the NAPLAN* paper, which will have about 50 questions. This means you will have less than a minute per answer.
- ✳ The paper is divided into two parts, which are worth equal marks. Aim to spend 20 minutes on each part.
- ✳ Work steadily through the questions, without rushing or dawdling. Don't be put off by an answer that seems too obvious or too simple.
- ✳ Start at question 1 and work through the questions in order. If you jump about too much, you risk accidentally missing a question.
- ✳ Temporarily skip any questions that you cannot do, rather than spending a long time on them. You might run out of time to do the easier questions!
- ✳ After you have worked through all the questions, return to any that you skipped earlier and have another go at answering them.

Review:

- ✳ Go back and check your answers if you have time at the end.
- ✳ Don't change an answer unless you are sure it is wrong!

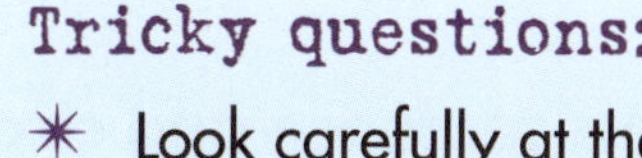

Tricky questions:

- ✳ Look carefully at the answers. Are there any that you know are wrong? Change them!
- ✳ If you can't answer a difficult question — guess!

*This is not an officially endorsed publication of the NAPLAN program and is produced by Pascal Press independently of Australian Governments.

PRE-TEST

This pre-test can help identify areas of weakness that need extra attention. The unit or units in this book that each question relates to are identified.

SPELLING

Each sentence has one word that is incorrect. Write the correct spelling in the box.

1 Some people say that nothing is inpossible. *(Unit 1)*

2 This is the happyest day of my life. *(Unit 2)*

3 Jemma caught a train to go to soccer traning. *(Units 3 & 4)*

4 The wicked wichs cast some spells. *(Units 5 & 6)*

5 Mushrooms don't come from plants with leafs; rather they are fungi. *(Units 7 & 8)*

GRAMMAR

Underline the noun group and circle the adjective group in this sentence.

6 The man with black boots entered the damp, dark cave. *(Units 9 & 10)*

Underline the adverbial in this sentence.

7 Leon has been learning the piano since he was four years old. *(Unit 11)*

For questions 8 to 10, shade the bubble of the word that completes each sentence correctly.

8 The children walked carefully ________ the road.

- ⬭ in
- ⬭ on
- ⬭ across
- ⬭ through *(Unit 12)*

9 I am ________ late for work today.

- ⬭ run
- ⬭ ran
- ⬭ runs
- ⬭ running *(Unit 13)*

10 The children ________ cricket after school.

- ⬭ play
- ⬭ plays *(Unit 14)*

11 **Underline the main clause in this sentence and circle the subordinating conjunction.**

The gardener hummed a tune while mowing the lawn. *(Units 15 & 16)*

PRE-TEST

PUNCTUATION

For questions 12 to 15, shade the bubble of the sentence with correct punctuation.

- ⬭ Fiona Zayn and Liam, want to be in a rock band, when they grow up.
- ⬭ Fiona, Zayn and Liam want to be in a rock band when they grow up.
- ⬭ Fiona, Zayn and Liam want to be in a rock band. When they grow up.
- ⬭ Fiona Zayn and Liam. Want to be in a rock band, when they grow up.

(Units 17 & 18)

- ⬭ "Can you hear me now? Rick asked".
- ⬭ "Can you hear me now Rick asked?"
- ⬭ "Can you hear me now?" Rick asked.
- ⬭ "Can you hear me now"? Rick asked. *(Units 19 & 20)*

- ⬭ Come and meet my co-workers: Ali, David and Emma.
- ⬭ Come and meet my coworkers: Ali, David and Emma.
- ⬭ Come and meet my co-workers; Ali, David and Emma.
- ⬭ Come and meet my coworkers; Ali, David and Emma. *(Units 21 & 22)*

- ⬭ Its time you gave the dog its lunch.
- ⬭ It's time you gave the dog it's lunch.
- ⬭ Its time you gave the dog it's lunch.
- ⬭ It's time you gave the dog its lunch. *(Units 23 & 24)*

MARKING GRID

Question	Unit	Skill	Correct/Incorrect
1	1	Prefixes	
2	2	Suffixes	
3	4	Rules for vowels	
4	5	Rules for consonants	
5	8	Uncommon plurals	
6	9 & 10	Noun and adjective groups	
7	11	Adverbials	
8	12	Articles and prepositions	
9	13	Verbs and tenses	
10	14	Subject and verb agreement	
11	15 & 16	Main and subordinate clauses & subordinating conjunctions	
12	18	Commas	
13	19	Quotations marks	
14	22	Colons and semi-colons	
15	23 & 24	Apostrophes	
TOTAL			

PREFIXES

SPELLING

A prefix is a group of letters added to the beginning of a word. It makes a new word.

Often the new word has the opposite meaning to the base word.

un + true = *untrue*

dis + able = *disable*

im + possible = *impossible*

The prefix 're' often means something is done again or repeated.

re + visit = *revisit*

Common prefixes include:
de, dis, il, im, in, ir, re, un.

Hint: sometimes the last letter of the prefix is the same as the first letter of the base word.

legal *illegal*

regular *irregular*

But this is not always the case!

reliable *unreliable*

When adding a prefix, the spelling of the base word does not change.

We practise

Write the circled word in the box with the correct prefix.

I had to disbuckle my little sister when the car stopped.	unbuckle
It is unexcusable to shout at your parents.	inexcusable
Sara will need to unconsider which sport to play.	reconsider
Our coach told us to run in an unclockwise direction.	anticlockwise

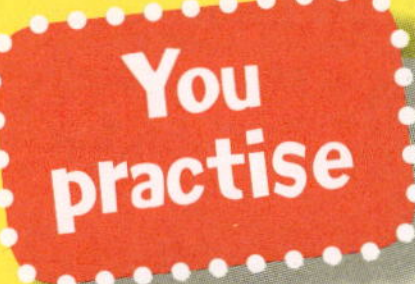

Write the circled word in the box with the correct prefix.

1 It was an inpossible task.

2 This will put you at a distinct unadvantage.

3 The answer given was unlogical.

4 The dress code for the party was unformal.

5 Nick was often disunderstood.

You practise

One word is incorrect. Write it in the box with the correct prefix.

6 Helen's classwork is too disconsistent.

7 Meera didn't want to unplease her boss.

8 The monster couldn't be killed because it was unmortal.

9 Don't lose that book, it's disreplaceable!

10 Sean's lost dog finally reeappeared.

BOB time!

SUFFIXES

A suffix is a letter or group of letters added to the end of a word. It makes a new word.

Often the spelling of the base word does not change when a suffix is added.

use + ful = *useful*

However, sometimes the base word changes when a suffix is added.

If the last letter is a consonant and the second last letter a vowel, double the last letter.

run + ing = *running*

There are always exceptions to the rules – try not to be tricked!

When the last letter is y, change the y to i.

happy + est = *happiest*

When the last letter is a silent e, remove the e.

make + ing = *making*

Common suffixes include: s, es, ed, er, est, ful, ing, ish, ly, less.

We practise

Write the circled word in the box with the correct suffix.

I am the (younging) person in my family.	youngest
Simon left the room (quickful).	quickly
Toula and I (walkes) to school yesterday.	walked
The little puppy was (fretest) for its owner.	fretting

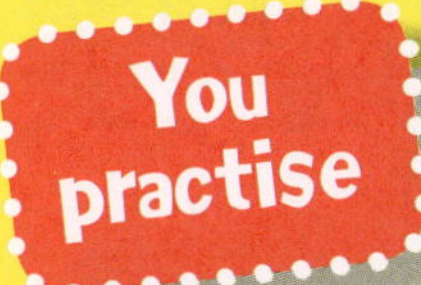

Write the circled word in the box with the correct suffix.

1 The teacher said my story was very interestful.

2 I am suntaned because I went to the beach.

3 The ground was quakeing under our feet.

4 That's the uglyful dog I've ever seen.

5 I am feeling hopful about the contest.

You practise

One word is incorrect. Write it in the box with the correct suffix.

6 Alice was jumped for joy when she heard the news.

7 That's the funniful joke I've ever heard!

8 Your new, blue dress is very beautiest.

9 Theo had a sheepful expression on his face.

10 That computer is too expensish.

BOB time!

HOMONYMS, HOMOGRAPHS and HOMOPHONES

Many words in English sound the same or similar, but mean **different** things.

Sounds very interesting!

Homonyms are words that have the same spelling and sound the same.

sign

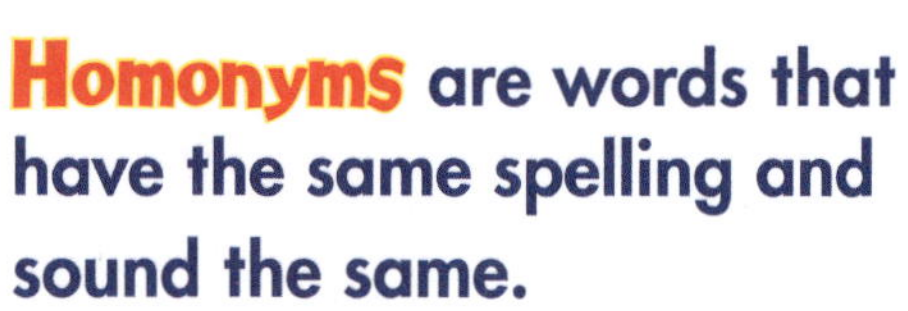

sign

Homographs are words that have the same spelling, but don't necessarily sound the same.

tear

tear

Homophones are words that have a different spelling, but sound the same.

see   sea

We practise

The spelling mistake in each sentence has been circled. Write the correct spelling in the box.

Andy (guest) the correct answer in the quiz.	guessed
We watched the polar (bares) from the underwater observatory.	bears
We throw all our fruit and vegetable (peal) in the compost bin.	peel
The tailor measured Sam's (waste) for the best fitting pants.	waist

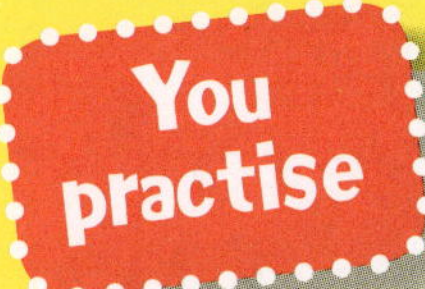

The spelling mistake in each sentence has been circled. Write the correct spelling in the box.

1 I have a big saw on my foot.

2 We are having chocolate moose for dessert.

3 Sarah couldn't wait for the male to be delivered.

4 It was there turn to go first.

5 Linda threw the ball threw the window.

You practise

Choose the correct word from the box to match the meanings. Write your answer on the line.

right, minute, lead, trip, wind

6	to go first	a type of metal	______
7	to stumble and fall	a journey	______
8	the correct answer	the opposite of left	______
9	to turn	a breeze	______
10	very small	60 seconds	______

RULES FOR VOWELS

For words with an ee sound, use i before e ...

thief, yield, believe

... except after c ...

ceiling, receive, deceit

... but there are always exceptions!

seize, protein, weird

When two vowels go walking, the first does the talking.

That is, the first vowel says its name ...

rain, beam, tie, toe, blue

... but there are always exceptions!

said, bread, cook, shoe, coin

The letter q is always followed by the letter u.

No exceptions.

Acronyms don't count as words when it comes to spelling rules e.g. *Qantas.*

quiet, quite, queen

The spelling mistake in each sentence has been circled. Write the correct spelling in the box.

Climate change

Most scientists beleive that global warming is taking place. | believe

Global warming refers to the heeting of the Earth's atmosphere. | heating

The climate is changing qwickly due to human activity. | quickly

Some areas are getting drier, while others are getting more rane. | rain

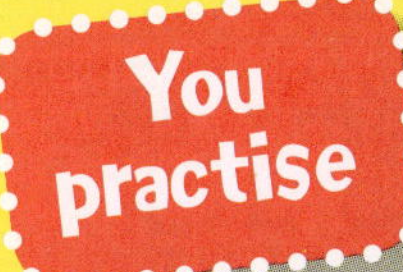

The spelling mistake in each sentence has been circled. Write the correct spelling in the box.

1. It is better to give than to (recieve.)
2. Gemma (floted) on her back in the swimming pool.
3. Andreas got all the answers right in the classroom (qwiz.)
4. An insect crawled across the pot plant's (lief.)
5. The (clowds) are dark and heavy, I think it will rain.

You practise

Each sentence has one word that is incorrect. Write the correct spelling in the box.

6. We drove past cows standing in a vast, green feild.
7. Giovanna went to the costume party dressed as a qween.
8. Russell's favourite snack is baked beens on toast.
9. Alison painted her toe nales with glossy, red polish.
10. You shoold come to the party, it's going to be fun.

Now try the spelling test on page 24!

BOB time!

RULES FOR CONSONANTS

These rules apply for consonants at the **end** of words.

If you hear a **k** after a short vowel, it is spelled **ck** ...

duck, back, sock

... but there are always exceptions!

disc, epic

If you hear a **ch** sound after a short vowel, it is spelled **tch** ...

hatch, witch

... but there are always exceptions!

rich, which

Rules can help, but keep exceptions in mind!

If you hear a **j** sound after a short vowel, it is spelled **dge** ...

badge, bridge, edge

... but if it comes after a long vowel, it is spelled **ge**.

rage, cage, siege

We practise

Each sentence has one word that is incorrect. Write the correct spelling in the box.

Wizard games

There are some magick tricks you can do at home.	magic
You will need a few simple tools, such as a dec of cards.	deck
A popular trick is to make a coin or a bage disappear.	badge
Be careful, people might think you are a wich!	witch

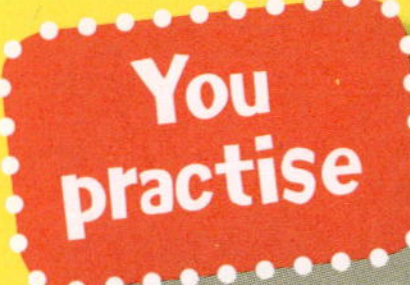

The words in the labels have the incorrect spelling. Write the correct spelling in the box.

nek 1 [ ]

badje 2 [ ]

socs 3 [ ]

backpak 4 [ ]

wach 5 [ ]

You practise

Each sentence has one word that is incorrect. Write the correct spelling in the box.

6 I am trying to teach my dog to fech the ball. [ ]

7 Dad warned us not to get too close to the cliff's edje. [ ]

8 The story's ending was tragick and it made everyone cry. [ ]

9 My uncle is engadged and will get married later this year. [ ]

10 Bella wanted to know which wich was which. [ ]

BOB time!

COMMON PLURALS

For many words, to make a plural you simply add **s** to the end of the word.

duck	*ducks*
building	*buildings*
table	*tables*

This is not always correct, however. If a word ends in **s**, **x**, **ch** or **sh**, add **es** to the end to make it plural.

bus	*buses*
fox	*foxes*
torch	*torches*
bush	*bushes*

The add **es** rule sometimes applies to words that end in **o** – but not always!

potato	*potatoes*
cello	*cellos*

Look carefully at the last letter of the word when making plurals.

We practise

Choose the correct spelling and write it in the box.

The foxes/foxs tried to sneak into the chicken coup.	foxes
We had to catch two trains/traines and two buses to get to our destination.	trains
Yianni ran away and hid behind some bush's/bushes.	bushes
We ate fish with fried potatoes, lettuce and tomatoes/tomatos.	tomatoes

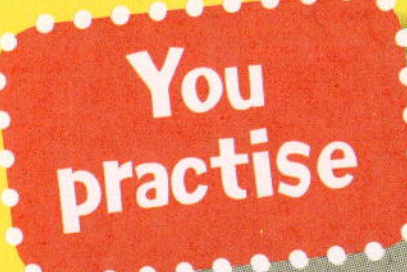

Which plural form is correct?
Write it in the box.

1 tomato — tomatoes/tomatos

2 leech — leechs/leeches

3 sheep — sheeps/sheep

4 class — classes/class

5 dish — dishs/dishes

You practise

Choose the correct spelling and write it in the box.

6 We visited several beautiful beachs/beaches during our holiday.

7 Mum is grumpy because she has to pay her taxes/taxs today.

8 Ina tried to get near the kangaroos/kangarooes, but they bounced away.

9 There are many types of viruses/virus's that can cause human disease.

10 There were so many hairbrushes/hairbrushs in the store, I couldn't decide which one to buy.

MORE COMMON PLURALS

If a word ends in 'y' and if the letter before the 'y' is a vowel, add '**s**'

toy *toys*

but if the letter before the 'y' is a consonant, remove the 'y' and add '**ies**'.

baby *babies*

If a word ends in 'f' and if you hear an 'f' sound in the plural, simply add '**s**'

reef *reefs*

but if you hear a 'v' sound in the plural, remove the 'f' and add '**ves**'.

wolf *wolves*

Some words change their vowel sound when they become a plural. They include:

man *men*
tooth *teeth*
goose *geese*

Some words don't change at all when they become a plural. They include:

sheep
deer
species

Pairs of things usually stay the same:

one pair of scissors
two pairs of scissors

Some words don't seem to follow any normal rules. You just need to learn and remember them!

child *children*
person *people*
ox *oxen*

Saying the word out loud can help you get the spelling right!

We practise

Choose the correct spelling and write it in the box.

The boys/boies ran across the playground. — boys

The thiefs/thieves were caught by the police and arrested. — thieves

Gooses/Geese used to be common for Christmas dinners. — Geese

We exercised so hard yesterday, we all have sore bodys/bodies today. — bodies

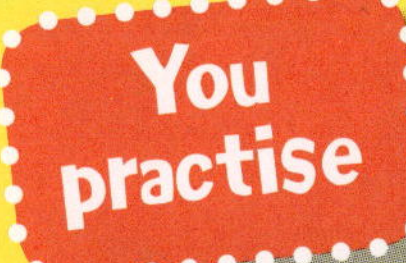

Which plural form is correct?
Write the correct word in the box.

1	loaf	loafs/loaves	
2	belly	bellys/bellies	
3	louse	louses/lice	
4	academy	academies/academys	
5	chef	chefs/cheves	

You practise

Choose the correct spelling and write it in the box.

6 This cereal is made of puvs/puffs of rice.

7 The stranded sailors soon ran out of supplies/supplys.

8 I love watching the leafs/leaves turn red in autumn.

9 It's better to make friends than enemies/enemys.

10 Luca bought two new pairs of jeans'/jeans.

BOB time!

UNIT 8

UNCOMMON PLURALS

English words that have their origin in foreign words can be confusing when they are made into plurals.

This is because they follow the rules of the foreign language, which can be hard to learn. Different spellings of the plurals are therefore often considered correct. For example, octopus is a Greek-based word. Acceptable plurals include octopi, octopodes, and octopuses!

You don't need to learn Latin and Greek! Use a dictionary when in doubt.

Latin-based words

If a word ends in 'us', change the ending to 'i'.

focus *foci*

If a word ends in 'um', change the ending to 'a'.

stadium *stadia*

If a word ends in 'ex', change the ending to 'ices'.

index *indices*

If a word ends in 'a', change the ending to 'ae'.

antenna *antennae*

Greek-based words

If a word ends in 'on', change the ending to 'a'.

criterion *criteria*

If a word ends in 'is', change the ending to 'es'.

crisis *crises*

We practise

Choose the most correct spelling and write it in the box.
Hint: follow the rules given on page 22.

Financial crises/crisises are sweeping the world.	crises
An ant's antennas/antennae are an important sensory organ.	antennae
On what criterions/criteria will you judge the competition?	criteria
The syllabi/syllabuses for school subjects will soon change.	syllabi

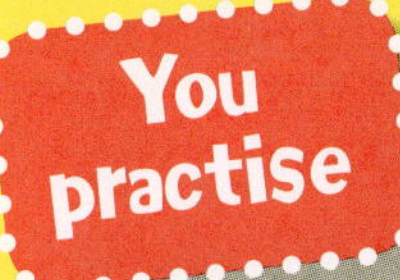

Which plural form is most correct? Write it in the box.
Hint: follow the rules given on page 22.

1 index indexes/indices

2 fungus fungi/funguses

3 analysis analysises/analyses

4 larva larvas/larvae

5 radius radii/radiuses

You practise

Choose the most correct spelling and write it in the box.
Hint: follow the rules given on page 22.

6 The dog sniffed some cacti/cactuses and prickled his nose.

7 Ria's sore throat was caused by bacteria/bacteriums.

8 Does anybody ever read the appendixes/appendices in the back of books?

9 Ghosts, UFOs and monsters are examples of strange phenomenums/phenomena.

10 Blue-green algae/algas in waterways may be toxic to humans.

Now try the spelling test on page 25!

BOB time!

You practise

SPELLING TEST 1

Do this test after completing Unit 4. Spend no more than 8 minutes on it.

The spelling mistake in each sentence has been circled. Write the correct spelling in the box.

1. Taking something without permission is (ilegal).

2. Can you smell the aroma of cakes (bakeing)?

3. The (disappearence) of the puppy caused much concern.

4. Tommy's little brother (bald) his eyes out when he scraped his knee.

5. Peter is so tall, his head nearly reaches the (cieling).

Each sentence has one word that is incorrect. Write the correct spelling in the box.

6. Ancient Greeks and Romans believed their gods were imortal and would never die.

7. We all felt dizzy after spinning around, but I think Lucy was the dizzyest.

8. That wobbly bike wheel is unrelyable and cannot be trusted.

9. When making bread, it is important to need the dough well.

10. Nobody scored a gole in last night's soccer match.

BOB time!

SPELLING TEST 2

Do this test after completing Unit 8. Spend no more than 8 minutes on it.

The spelling mistake in each sentence has been circled. Write the correct spelling in the box.

1. The wild dog was full of manick energy.

2. The race was cancelled because no one could find the stopwaches.

3. There are many advantadges to this approach.

4. Our holiday included a tour of churchs.

5. Many funguses are poisonous to human beings.

Each sentence has one word that is incorrect. Write the correct spelling in the box.

6. Ming's greatest dream is to work hard and be ritch.

7. The brave knight faced his enemy filled with couradge.

8. The babys in day care all started crying at once.

9. Mum bought a new set of expensive kitchen knifes.

10. Ryan's life seemed to be a series of crisises.

BOB time!

NOUN GROUPS

GRAMMAR

Nouns are naming words. They can name people, places, things or ideas.

Nouns can be the **subject** of a sentence (the person or thing doing something) or the **object** (the person or thing being acted on).

The extra words in a noun group are known as **descriptors**.

A noun group is a group of words based around a noun.

Noun groups are extra words that provide fuller descriptions of a person, place, thing or idea.

The extra words can come **before** or **after** the noun that they describe.

The extra words in a noun group can be:

* articles (the, a, an) e.g. **the** ball
* numbers or quantities e.g. **two** girls, **many** birds
* possessives (words that show ownership) e.g. **Ron's** book
* other nouns e.g. the cat in the **tree**
* adjectives e.g. **brown** trousers.

Underline a noun group around the circled noun.

The woman with long, black hair was drinking coffee.

A small group of children were playing outside.

The old man's house was in need of repair.

The car in the showroom was very expensive.

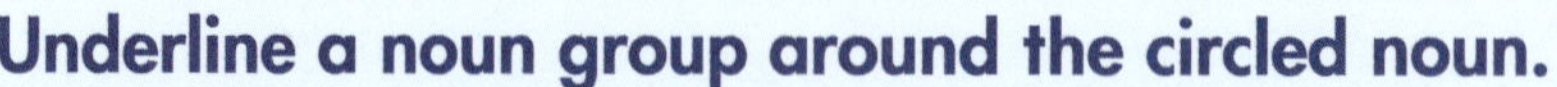

You practise

Underline a noun group around the circled noun in each sentence.

1 Five seagulls fought for the scraps of bread.

2 The long wooden table was covered with a clean, white tablecloth.

3 The long wooden table was covered with a clean, white tablecloth.

4 A couple of singers performed at the school down the road.

5 A couple of singers performed at the school down the road.

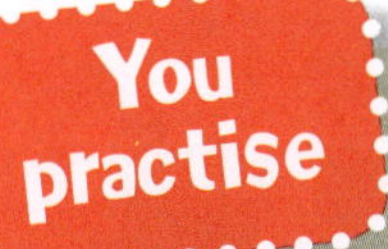

Which word or words form a noun group?
Shade ONE bubble in each question.

6 **The frightened cat ran away.**

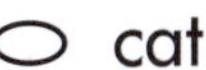
- cat
- ran
- ran away
- the frightened cat

7 **The man with a walking stick nearly fell over.**

- man
- walking stick
- the man with a walking stick
- nearly fell over

8 **The dogs in the street began to bark.**

- dogs
- street
- began to bark
- the dogs in the street

9 **Twelve children went to the party.**

- children
- party
- twelve children
- to the party

BOB time!

ADJECTIVE GROUPS

An adjective is a word that describes a noun.

The **happy baby** smiled.

adjective → happy; noun → baby

Adjective groups bring writing to life!

An adjective group is a group of words that give more detailed information about the noun. They make the writing more vivid. Adjective groups can contain one or more adjectives.

The adjective group can come **before** or **after** the noun that it is describing.

The **plump, blonde, happy baby** smiled.

adjective group → plump, blonde, happy; noun → baby

The **movie** was **too long and dull.**

noun → movie; adjective group → too long and dull

Where a string of adjectives is written one after the other in a list, a comma is placed between them.

We practise

Find the adjectives that describe the circled noun and write them in the box.

The woman brushed her long, silky (hair). — long, silky

The young and beautiful (woman) brushed her hair. — young, beautiful

Find the adjective group that describes the circled noun and write it in the box.

The (roller-coaster) at the show was scary and fun! — scary and fun

We watched the huge and hungry (crocodile) as it jumped out of the water. — huge and hungry

You practise

Find the adjective or adjectives that describe the circled noun. Write them in the box.

1 The majestic (eagle) soared across the blue sky.

2 The majestic eagle soared across the blue (sky).

3 The threadbare (rug) was gritty and dirty.

You practise

Find the adjective group that describes the circled noun. Write it in the box.

4 The damp, dark (cave) was closed to the public.

5 The (spider) was big and hairy and it climbed up my leg.

You practise

Which words form an adjective group? Shade ONE bubble in each question.

6 **Mum made steaming hot soup when I was ill.**

- ○ soup
- ○ hot
- ○ steaming hot
- ○ I was ill

7 **Huan bit into the sweet, juicy watermelon.**

- ○ Huan bit
- ○ watermelon
- ○ sweet, juicy
- ○ bit into the

8 **Pandora opened the big mysterious box.**

- ○ opened
- ○ box
- ○ big mysterious
- ○ Pandora opened

9 **The boy with the green eyes is not coming today.**

- ○ the boy
- ○ not coming
- ○ not coming today
- ○ with the green eyes

BOB time!

ADVERBIALS

An adverb is a word that describes a verb (a verb is an action word). Adverbs show how the action was performed.

Meredith **walked quickly.**

verb adverb

An adverbial is a group of words that describes the verb. Adverbials provide more detailed information about the action or event.

Adverbials can show **how** the action was performed, **when** or **where** it happened, **why** it happened, and/or for **how long**.

Meredith **walked for over one hour.**

verb adverbial

We practise

Underline the adverbial in each sentence.

Fiona was sleeping on the spare mattress.

We bought a new car because our old one kept breaking down.

Jemma has been playing soccer since she was four years old.

Brush and floss your teeth before you go to the dentist.

You practise

Underline the adverbial in each sentence.

I love walking along the beach.

Indira hammered in the nail with all her strength.

Eat your dinner before you have dessert.

Yesterday I hurt my foot.

I found the lost library book under my bed.

You practise

Which words form an adverbial group?
Shade ONE bubble in each question.

Mum made steaming hot soup when I was ill.

- ⬭ steaming hot soup
- ⬭ hot soup
- ⬭ Mum made
- ⬭ when I was ill

I didn't go to school because it was Saturday.

- ⬭ school
- ⬭ didn't go
- ⬭ Saturday
- ⬭ because it was Saturday

The boy with the green eyes is not coming today.

- ⬭ the boy
- ⬭ not coming
- ⬭ today
- ⬭ with the green eyes

The cake is baking in the oven.

- ⬭ the cake
- ⬭ baking
- ⬭ in the oven
- ⬭ the cake is baking

BOB time!

ARTICLES and PREPOSITIONS

Articles describe nouns. There are only three articles in English: a, an, the.

The **definite** article 'the' refers to a specific person, place or thing.

*Mum wishes she had learned to play **the** piano when she was young.*

The **indefinite** articles 'a' and 'an' do not refer to a specific person, place or thing. 'An' is used for words beginning with a vowel.

*Mum wishes she had learned **a** musical instrument when she was young.*

Don't end a sentence with a preposition!

Avoid this trap:
'different to' and 'different than' are often considered wrong. 'Different from' is correct.

Prepositions are words that give the position or location of something.

They are usually used with pronouns or nouns.

The cat is balancing **on** the fence.
↑ **preposition**

Prepositions can also tell us when something happens.

The neighbour's dog always barks **at** night.
↑ **preposition**

Common prepositions include: on, in, above, under, beside, between, with, until, always, never.

We practise

Choose the correct word from the list to fill each gap and write it in the box.

in, an, a, into

Marie wants to be ____ doctor when she grows up. [a]

Steve asked the doctor whether he will need ____ anaesthetic. [an]

The burglar escaped by jumping out of a window and ____ a waiting car. [into]

You practise

Choose a preposition from the list to fill each gap and write it in the box.

under, behind, on, in, over

1. The cat jumped _____ the fence. [ ]

2. The mouse was hiding _____ the wardrobe. [ ]

3. I watched a documentary _____ television. [ ]

4. Some people say it is unlucky to walk _____ a ladder. [ ]

5. I didn't want to get out of bed _____ the morning. [ ]

You practise

Which word completes the sentence correctly? Shade ONE bubble.

6. **I read 'Harry Potter' and I think it is _____ best book I have ever read.**
   - ○ a
   - ○ an
   - ○ the

7. **Can you go to the store and buy me _____ bag of apples?**
   - ○ a
   - ○ an
   - ○ the

8. **The old lady needed help to get _____ the road.**
   - ○ under
   - ○ across
   - ○ through
   - ○ in

9. **Mei-Lien was very tired and fell asleep _____ class.**
   - ○ on
   - ○ at
   - ○ during
   - ○ over

10. **Lots of dust gathered on the floor _____ my bed.**
    - ○ in
    - ○ under
    - ○ through
    - ○ at

Now try the grammar test on page 42!

BOB time!

VERBS and TENSES

Verbs are **action** words e.g. swim, eat, cry.

Tenses tell **when** the action in the sentence or story is taking place. It may be in the past, present or future.

Past tense

Sometimes 'ed' is added to the base word e.g. walk – *walked*.

Alex *walked* down the street.

Sometimes the base word changes completely e.g. write – *wrote* – *written*.

Alex *wrote* a letter.

Alex *has written* a letter.

Sometimes verbs change their form depending on the tense. A suffix might be added (*ed*, *ing*) or the verb might change completely.

Present tense

Sometimes 's' is added to the base word e.g. walk – *walks*.

Alex *walks* down the street.

Sometimes 'ing' is added to the base word e.g. walk – *walking*.

Alex *is walking* down the street.

Future tense

The words 'will' or 'is going to' often come before the verb.

Alex *will walk* down the street.

Alex *is going to walk* down the street.

Verbs that change completely depending on tense are known as **irregular** verbs.

Which word or words complete the sentence correctly? Shade ONE bubble in each question.

Rose ____ into the apple and her tooth fell out.

- ○ is biting
- ● bit
- ○ will bite
- ○ bite

Ahmed has ____ a beautiful picture to enter a competition.

- ○ painting
- ○ will paint
- ● painted
- ○ paint

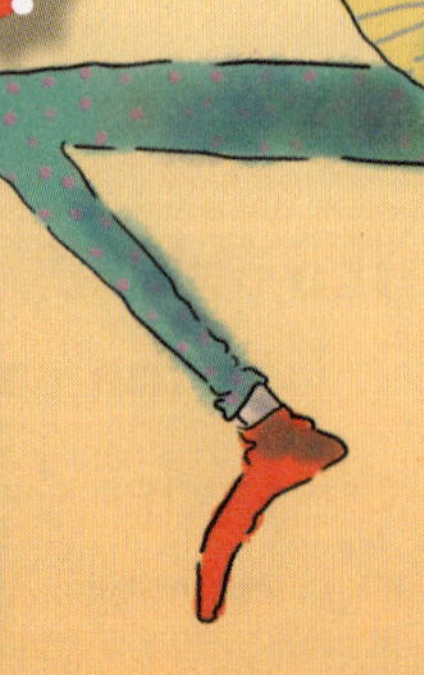

You practise

Which word or words complete the sentence correctly? Shade ONE bubble in each question.

1. **Charlotte _____ over yesterday.**
   - ○ falls
   - ○ fell
   - ○ felled
   - ○ is falling

2. **Jonathon is _____ for dinner tonight.**
   - ○ came
   - ○ come
   - ○ coming
   - ○ will come

3. **Magda decided to _____ her bike to school every day.**
   - ○ rode
   - ○ ridden
   - ○ riding
   - ○ ride

4. **Sasha has lots of trouble _____ up her mind.**
   - ○ making
   - ○ made
   - ○ will make
   - ○ has made

You practise

Which word completes the sentence correctly? Shade ONE bubble.

5. **Ibrahim _____ his homework before he had dinner.**
   - ○ done
   - ○ did
   - ○ doing
   - ○ does

6. **Alessio screamed when he _____ the apple and found a worm.**
   - ○ bited
   - ○ bit
   - ○ bitten
   - ○ bite

7. **Sally cried until she thought her heart would _____.**
   - ○ broke
   - ○ broken
   - ○ break
   - ○ breaks

8. **I should have _____ more food for lunch.**
   - ○ brought
   - ○ bring
   - ○ brung
   - ○ bringing

9. **I think I might have _____ a cold.**
   - ○ catch
   - ○ catched
   - ○ caught
   - ○ catching

BOB time!

SUBJECT and VERB AGREEMENT

Sentences contain a **subject** (a person or thing that does something) and a **verb** (an action word).

The subject and verb must agree.

Unlike nouns, you don't add 's' to a verb to make it plural. Often it's the opposite!

A **singular** subject must have a singular verb.

The **girl runs** quickly.

Singular subject Singular verb

Plural subjects must have plural verbs.

The **girls run** quickly.

Plural subject Plural verb

Watch out for the following:

One subject AND another – use a plural verb.

*The dog and the cat **chase** the mouse.*

One subject OR another – use a singular verb.

*The dog or the cat **chases** the mouse.*

Circle the correct verb so that the subject and verb agree.

Ahmed is/are one of the best students in the class.

The colours of the rainbow is/are beautiful.

Joseph want/wants to go to the park.

Joseph and Ron want/wants to go to the park.

Either Joseph or Ron want/wants to go to the park.

We practise

You practise

Which word completes the sentence correctly?
Shade ONE bubble in each question.

The girls _____ after the ball.

- ○ run
- ○ runs

The girl _____ after the ball.

- ○ run
- ○ runs

Jamie and Georgio _____ arriving today.

- ○ is
- ○ are

Either Jamie or Georgio _____ arriving today.

- ○ is
- ○ are

The can of baked beans _____ on the shelf.

- ○ sits
- ○ sit

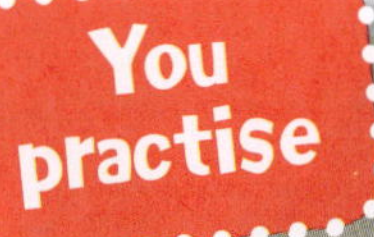

Which word completes the sentence correctly?
Shade ONE bubble in each question.

Mathematics _____ my favourite subject.

- ○ is
- ○ are

The scissors _____ on the table.

- ○ is
- ○ are

We _____ told to go home early.

- ○ was
- ○ were

I _____ catching the train tomorrow.

- ○ am
- ○ are

We _____ catching the train tomorrow.

- ○ am
- ○ are

BOB time!

MAIN and SUBORDINATE CLAUSES

A **clause** is a group of words that form part of a sentence.

Incomplete sentences are known as **fragments**.

The following sentence has two clauses: a **main** clause and a **subordinate** clause.

Eric ate his breakfast **before he walked to school.**

Main clause **Subordinate clause**

A complete thought that can form a sentence all by itself.

'Eric ate his breakfast' can be a complete sentence.

Subordinate clause

Not a complete thought, and it cannot stand alone as a sentence.

Instead, it **gives more information about the main clause.**
'Before he walked to school' is not a complete sentence.

Main clauses often come first in sentences, but not always. If a subordinate clause comes first, insert a comma to separate the clauses.

Before he walked to school, Eric ate his breakfast.

Circle the main clause and underline the subordinate clause in each sentence.

Although it's cold, I still want to play outside.

She swept the floor because it was dirty.

There is no point in starting until everyone is here.

Since I knitted that scarf, I'd like to wear it.

You practise

Underline the main clause in each sentence.

1. The car would not start because the battery was flat.

2. You cannot enter the swimming carnival unless you can swim.

3. Nelson swept the floor because it was dirty.

4. After we have lunch, we'll go for a walk.

5. Once she has saved enough money, Gina is going overseas.

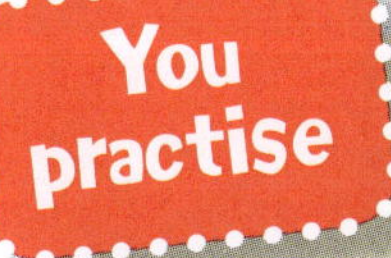

Underline the subordinate clause in each sentence.

6. The car would not start because the battery was flat.

7. You cannot enter the swimming carnival unless you can swim.

8. Nelson swept the floor because it was dirty.

9. After we have lunch, we'll go for a walk.

10. Once she has saved enough money, Gina is going overseas.

BOB time!

SUBORDINATING CONJUNCTIONS

Conjunctions join two clauses, or parts of a sentence. They help show how the ideas in the clauses are linked or related.

Common subordinating conjunctions include: after, although, as, because, before, if, once, since, unless, until, when, where, while.

Subordinating conjunctions link main clauses to subordinate clauses.

I ate some breakfast before I walked to school.

Main clause | **Subordinating conjunction** | **Subordinate clause**

You can re-write this sentence putting the subordinate clause first.

Before I walked to school, I ate some breakfast.

Subordinating conjunction | **Subordinate clause** | **Main clause**

Did you notice the comma in the re-written sentence?

We practise

Underline the subordinating conjunction in each sentence.

I'll look after your dog while you are away.

He swept the floor because it was dirty.

There is no point in starting until everyone is here.

Before you leave, you have to tidy up your room.

You practise

Pick a word from the list below to complete each sentence correctly. Write the word in the box.

after, until, while, because, if

1. Brush your teeth _____ eating lollies.
2. It won't be over _____ the last person sings.
3. Mum cooked dinner _____ I set the table.
4. _____ it started to rain, we had to go inside.
5. It will break _____ you push it too hard.

You practise

Which word completes the sentence correctly? Shade ONE bubble in each question.

6. **William will go to his friend's house _____ school today.**
   - ○ while
   - ○ unless
   - ○ until
   - ○ after

7. **Ali drank some cocoa _____ he went to bed.**
   - ○ until
   - ○ before
   - ○ after
   - ○ because

8. **_____ you hurry up, you will be late.**
   - ○ Unless
   - ○ As
   - ○ If
   - ○ Because

9. **The music was too loud _____ Zhu turned it down.**
   - ○ so
   - ○ because
   - ○ while
   - ○ if

10. **_____ my dog slobbers a lot, I still like to cuddle him.**
    - ○ If
    - ○ When
    - ○ Although
    - ○ Until

Now try the grammar test on page 43!

BOB time!

You practise

GRAMMAR TEST 1

Do this test after completing Unit 12. Spend no more than 6 minutes on this test.

Shade ONE bubble for each question to show your answer.

In questions 1 and 2, which word or words form a noun group?

1 Dad's car would not start.

- ⬭ start
- ⬭ would not start
- ⬭ car
- ⬭ Dad's car

2 The boy with the blue T-shirt fell over and scraped his knee.

- ⬭ boy
- ⬭ the boy with the blue T-shirt
- ⬭ fell over
- ⬭ scraped his knee

In questions 3 and 4, which word or words form an adjective group?

3 Last summer was hotter than usual.

- ⬭ summer
- ⬭ last summer
- ⬭ hotter than usual
- ⬭ usual

4 The students, in full school uniform, went on an excursion.

- ⬭ students
- ⬭ school uniform
- ⬭ in full school uniform
- ⬭ an excursion

In questions 5 and 6, which word or words form an adverbial?

5 Susan fell down the stairs and grazed her knee.

- ⬭ Susan fell
- ⬭ down the stairs
- ⬭ and grazed
- ⬭ grazed her knee

6 The school holidays start next week.

- ⬭ school
- ⬭ school holidays
- ⬭ start
- ⬭ next week

In questions 7 and 8, which word completes the sentence correctly?

7 It was hard to see _____ the grimy window.

- ⬭ under
- ⬭ on
- ⬭ across
- ⬭ through

8 The new-born puppies snuggled _____ the warm blanket.

- ⬭ through
- ⬭ over
- ⬭ under
- ⬭ off

BOB time!

GRAMMAR TEST 2

Do this test after completing Unit 16. Spend no more than 6 minutes on this test.

For questions 1 to 6, shade ONE bubble to show your answer.

Which word completes the sentence correctly?

1 **The glass fell on the floor and _____.**
- ○ broke
- ○ broken
- ○ break
- ○ breaks

2 **Come over here and _____ a sticker.**
- ○ chose
- ○ chosen
- ○ choose
- ○ chosing

3 **My favourite dessert _____ apple pie.**
- ○ is
- ○ are

4 **Apple pies _____ my favourite dessert.**
- ○ is
- ○ are

5 **Matt did not make the team _____ he tried his best.**
- ○ if
- ○ once
- ○ although
- ○ therefore

6 **You might get cavities _____ you don't brush your teeth.**
- ○ until
- ○ although
- ○ once
- ○ if

Underline the main clause in the sentence.

7 Chris kept watch while Tom and Jack went to sleep.

Underline the subordinate clause in the sentence.

8 Whenever she hears music, Carol starts to sing along.

BOB time!

UNIT 17

CAPITAL LETTERS and FULL STOPS

Capital letter ABC

When starting a sentence

When using proper nouns

Full stop .

When ending most sentences

Proper nouns are words that name specific people and places.

Thomas, Australia, Mars

Common nouns, on the other hand, refer to **general** people and places, such as *girl, city, country*.

The names of days, holidays and months are proper nouns, and should start with a capital letter.

Monday, Christmas, September

Languages are also proper nouns.

English, Greek, Cantonese

The main words in book, movie and song titles should also have capital letters.

Harry Potter and the Philosopher's Stone

Capital letters and full stops show where sentences begin and end, making them easier to understand.

We practise

Highlight capital letters and full stops in this story.

My best friend's name is Chloe. We live near each other and go to the same school. We usually walk to school but sometimes Mum drives us, especially if it is raining. On the weekends, Chloe and I like to go to Ramsgate, our favourite beach. We swim for hours and have races along the sand. I wish we could take my dog Sandy with us, but dogs aren't allowed at our beach. Sometimes after swimming we get to go to our favourite restaurant, The Ramsgate Palace. Chloe's brother has promised to teach me how to ride on a bodyboard. We start next Saturday.

You practise

Which two words should begin with a capital letter?
Shade TWO bubbles in each question.

Anna has a pet cat called socks and will buy him a toy mouse next saturday.

She bought her cat from pet paradise, her local pet store.

Mum, ben and i are going on holiday next week.

We are going to cairns and we leave here on monday.

Which sentence has the correct punctuation?
Shade ONE bubble in each question.

- ⬭ Louise didn't go to School. Today her head aches and her throat is sore.
- ⬭ Louise didn't go to School today. her head aches and her throat is sore.
- ⬭ Louise didn't go to school today. her head aches and her throat is sore.
- ⬭ Louise didn't go to school today. Her head aches and her throat is sore.

- ⬭ Dad went fishing on sunday I went with him. And we caught a big fish.
- ⬭ Dad went fishing on sunday I went with him and we caught a big Fish.
- ⬭ Dad went fishing on Sunday. I went with him and we caught a big fish.
- ⬭ Dad went fishing on Sunday. I went with him and we caught a big Fish.

- ⬭ Yesterday we went to Bondi Beach. We spent the whole day swimming.
- ⬭ Yesterday we went to bondi beach. We spent the whole day swimming.
- ⬭ Yesterday we went to bondi beach we spent the whole day swimming.
- ⬭ Yesterday we went to Bondi beach we spent the whole day swimming.

BOB time!

COMMAS

Comma	,	When pausing in a sentence When separating items in a list When separating words that interrupt the flow of a sentence When a main clause follows a subordinate clause

Read the sentence out loud and consider inserting a comma where you need to take a breath.

Highlight the commas in this story.

Jimmy told everyone in the class that Rosie had a crush on Evan, the school captain. Even Sarah, her best friend, believed it. Rosie denied everything.

On Valentine's Day, Jimmy gave Rosie a card, pretending it was from Evan. The card read, "Roses are red, violets are blue. Rosie my love, you're too good to be true."

Rosie, however, was not fooled. She sent a card back to Jimmy that read, "Roses are red, violets are blue. I know who likes Rosie, yes it is you!"

His face turning red as roses, Jimmy's teasing suddenly stopped!

You practise

Where does the missing comma (,) go?
Shade ONE bubble in each question.

1. I want to go to the park ○ after school ○ today ○ but ○ it is too cold.

2. Unless you eat ○ your vegetables ○ there ○ will be ○ no dessert.

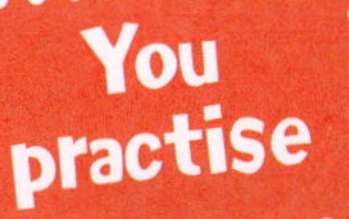

You practise

Where do the missing commas (,) go?
Shade TWO bubbles in each question.

3. I am ○ as you ○ can see ○ tall ○ for my age.

4. The Australian ○ English ○ and American ○ flags are red ○ white and blue.

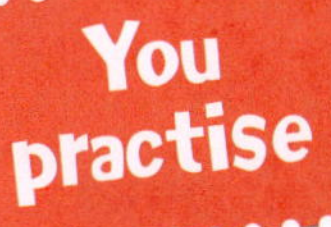

You practise

Which sentence has the correct punctuation?
Shade ONE bubble in each question.

5.
- ○ Although frightening most earthquakes, do not cause any damage.
- ○ Although frightening, most earthquakes do not cause any damage.
- ○ Although frightening, most earthquakes, do not cause any damage.
- ○ Although frightening most earthquakes, do not cause, any damage.

6.
- ○ The earthquake made my bed, desk and wardrobe tremble.
- ○ The earthquake made my bed, desk and wardrobe, tremble.
- ○ The earthquake, made my bed desk and wardrobe, tremble.
- ○ The earthquake, made my bed desk and wardrobe tremble.

7.
- ○ The whole house shook but, luckily nothing was broken.
- ○ The whole house shook, but luckily nothing was broken.
- ○ The whole house shook but luckily, nothing, was broken.
- ○ The whole house shook but luckily nothing, was broken.

BOB time!

QUOTATION MARKS

Quotation marks are also called speech marks. They are used for direct speech, that is, for actual words spoken. They always come in pairs and they look like this, “ when someone starts talking and, ” after they finish.

Quotation marks are only used for direct speech – not when someone is thinking.

Direct speech starts with a capital letter. Punctuation for the speaker's words (e.g. commas, question marks) always goes **inside** the quotation marks. Do not add extra punctuation directly after the quotation marks.

The speaker's name goes **outside** the quotation marks, either before or after the speech. Often a comma separates the speaker's words from other parts of the sentence.

Highlight the correct punctuation for direct speech in each sentence.

Connie said, “We are going to the pool today.”

“This is fantastic!” shouted Sanjiv.

“Can I have another biscuit please?” Aimee asked.

The canteen lady asked, “Do you have any smaller notes?”

“Take your time and do not rush,” Richard said.

You practise

Where do the missing quotation marks (" ") go? Shade TWO bubbles in each question.

1. ○ We need to repaint the kitchen, ○ Mum ○ said to Dad. ○

2. ○ How much do you think that will cost us ○ ? ○ Dad asked. ○

3. ○ Mum shouted, ○ Great, I knew you'd say yes ○ ! ○

4. ○ Dad muttered, ○ Maybe I'll try washing the walls tomorrow ○ . ○

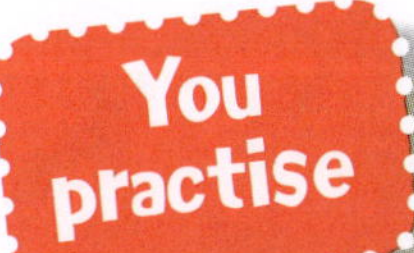

Which sentence has the correct punctuation? Shade ONE bubble in each question.

5.
- ○ "Is this the correct answer"? Mia asked.
- ○ "Is this the correct answer? Mia asked?"
- ○ "Is this the correct answer?" Mia asked.
- ○ "Is this the correct answer. Mia asked"?

6.
- ○ "Careful, you nearly hit me in the head with that ball Matthew shouted!"
- ○ "Careful, you nearly hit me in the head with that ball!" Matthew shouted.
- ○ "Careful, you nearly hit me in the head with that ball! Matthew shouted".
- ○ "Careful, you nearly hit me in the head with that ball"! Matthew shouted.

7.
- ○ "The teacher asked Did you remember to do your homework?"
- ○ "The teacher asked, Did you remember to do your homework?"
- ○ The teacher asked, "Did you remember to do your homework?"
- ○ The teacher asked, "Did you remember to do your homework"?

BOB time!

QUESTION MARKS and EXCLAMATION MARKS

Question mark ?

At the end of a direct question
e.g. *What did you have for lunch?*

Not used for indirect questions
e.g. *I asked you what you had for lunch.*

Exclamation mark !

At the end of sentences that are commands (an order to do something)
e.g. *Get dressed!*

or exclamations (something showing strong feelings) e.g. *I'm so excited!*

Try not to overuse exclamation marks! They aren't always necessary!!!

Highlight question marks and exclamation marks in this play script.

Man: *(approaches a woman in the street)* Excuse me, Madam, can you please tell me the time?

Woman: *(angrily)* What did you say?

Man: I asked you to tell me the time.

Woman: Well, that's a bit rude, isn't it?

Man: *(shocked)* Why is it rude?

Woman: Do I look like the sort of person who can tell the time?

Man: *(slowly)* Well … you are wearing a watch.

Woman: *(shouting)* That doesn't mean I go around giving complete strangers the time of day! What sort of person do you think I am?

Man: Forget it. Actually, I can tell **you** the time, if you like.

Woman: What do you mean?

Man: Time for you to see a doctor, lady, you're nuts!

You practise

Shade ONE bubble in each question to show where the missing question mark (?) should go.

"Did you hear ○ something ○ ○ " Ryan asked ○

2 Henry ○ asked ○ "Where are my socks ○ ○ "

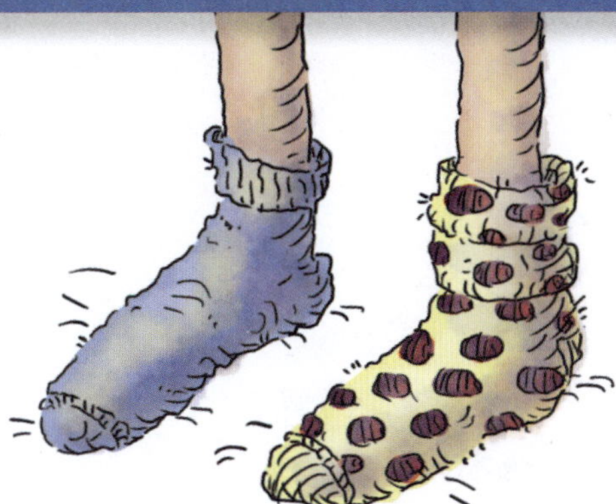

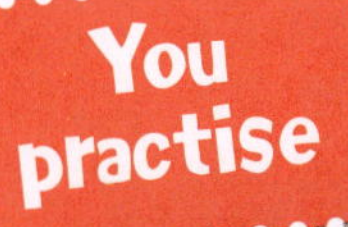

Shade ONE bubble in each question to show where the missing exclamation mark (!) should go.

"I want to go home right now ○ ○ " Sasha ○ shouted ○

Look out ○ there's an angry ○ dog ○ behind you ○

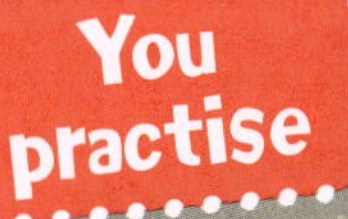

Which sentence has the correct punctuation? Shade ONE bubble in each question.

- ○ "What time does school finish on sports days?" Shirley asked.
- ○ "What time does school finish on sports days!" Shirley asked.
- ○ "What time does school finish on sports days," Shirley asked?
- ○ "What time does school finish on sports days," Shirley asked!

- ○ Shirley wondered what time school finishes on sports days?
- ○ Shirley wondered what time school finishes on sports days!
- ○ Shirley wondered what time school finishes on sports days.
- ○ Shirley wondered what time school finishes? on sports days.

- ○ It is my birthday tomorrow! and I can't wait to see my presents.
- ○ It is my birthday tomorrow and I can't wait to see my presents?
- ○ It is my birthday tomorrow and I can't wait to see my presents!
- ○ It is my birthday tomorrow! and I can't wait to see my presents?

BOB time!

Now try the punctuation test on page 60!

HYPHENS and DASHES

Hyphen - **Join compound words**
e.g. *long-term, good-natured*

Attach some prefixes
e.g. *ex-wife, anti-terrorism*, especially where a vowel repeats e.g. *co-owner*

To avoid confusion where the unhyphenated word means something else e.g. *re-cover, not recover*

Hyphens are within words and **dashes** are between words. They look similar, but dashes are longer.

Dash – **Two dashes** to separate interrupting words in a sentence e.g. *We are – or sometimes are – in the top maths group.*

One dash to show a change of thought or direction e.g. *I've always wanted a pet dog – and this year Mum bought a cat.*

We practise

Add hyphens and dashes to each sentence as needed.
Hint: you may need to add more than one in each sentence.

The good-looking actor smiled at the audience.

She spun anti-clockwise before re-entering the room.

I re-sent the letter yesterday, so please don't resent me!

I love the beach – sun, sand and water – it's my favourite place on Earth.

It looked like it was going to rain – but it snowed.

You practise

Add hyphens or dashes to each sentence as needed.
Hint: you may need to add more than one in each sentence.

1 My big brother is getting married, so soon I will have a sister in law.

2 Mum says her co workers are very nice.

3 My brothers Cody, Sam and Harry are all taller than me.

4 Re creation of the crime can help solve who did it.

5 I thought I knew the answer but clearly I was wrong.

You practise

Where does the missing hyphen (-) go?
Shade ONE bubble in each question.

6 We ○ are looking ○ for a long ○ term solution ○ to this problem.

7 Dad was ○ n't happy with the car's ○ shine so ○ he re ○ buffed it.

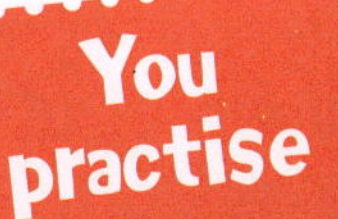

Where does the missing dash (–) go?
Shade ONE bubble.

8 "I wish you ○ would ○ oh never mind," ○ Rory ○ muttered.

Where do the missing dashes (–) go?
Shade TWO bubbles.

9 I need three ○ things ○ lettuce, tomato ○ and cucumber ○ to make a salad.

BOB time!

COLONS and SEMICOLONS

Colon :

Introduces a list of items
e.g. *She went to the supermarket and bought: eggs, flour and butter.*

Introduces an explanation
e.g. *pancake: a thin, flat cake of fried batter*

Look carefully at the symbols so that you don't mix them up.

Semicolon ;

Joins two main clauses that could otherwise be separate sentences.

It is used to show there is a relationship or link between the two clauses
e.g. *Sam's favourite colour is green; Naomi's favourite colour is blue.*

We practise

Circle the correct punctuation mark in each sentence.

The DJ played many great songs (:) ; hip-hop, rap and pop.

I know the answer to the maths question (:) ; it is 28.

Americans call it soccer : / (;) the British call it football.

Rania studied hard all year : (;) she got good marks in her school report.

You practise

Circle the correct punctuation mark in each sentence.

In my lunch box I have : / ; a sandwich, a banana and a packet of sultanas.

Stanley wants to be an author when he grows up : / ; he is a talented writer.

The Australian Coat of Arms has two native animals : / ; the kangaroo and the emu.

We all knew who would win the race : / ; Jasmin.

We are going to New Zealand this year : / ; my uncle is getting married in Wellington.

Which sentence has the correct punctuation?
Shade ONE bubble in each question.

- ⬭ For dinner last night: we had roast beef, potatoes and peas.
- ⬭ For dinner last night; we had roast beef, potatoes and peas.
- ⬭ For dinner last night we had; roast beef, potatoes and peas.
- ⬭ For dinner last night we had: roast beef, potatoes and peas.

- ⬭ It was zero degrees outside: Brian was worried he might get frostbite.
- ⬭ It was zero degrees outside; Brian was worried he might get frostbite.
- ⬭ It was zero degrees outside Brian was worried he might: get frostbite.
- ⬭ It was zero degrees outside Brian was worried he might; get frostbite.

- ⬭ Dingo a wild dog of Australia: having a reddish-brown or tan coat.
- ⬭ Dingo a wild dog of Australia; having a reddish-brown or tan coat.
- ⬭ Dingo: a wild dog of Australia, having a reddish-brown or tan coat.
- ⬭ Dingo: a wild dog of Australia having a reddish-brown or tan coat.

APOSTROPHES for CONTRACTIONS

Some words can be shortened or combined, making them quicker and easier to say and write. These are known as contractions.

Sometimes one word is contracted to make a shorter word.

cannot *can't*

More often, two words are contracted or combined into one word.

do not *don't*

Contractions make a sentence less formal. Use them when writing dialogue; it's how most people speak.

Avoid this common trap: It's is a contraction of it + is. It is not used to show ownership.

An apostrophe ' is used to show that the word is a contraction. It is put in the exact place where the letters have been left out.

Highlight the contractions in this story.

"**Don't** you think **you've** had enough cereal today?" Mum asked Aaron.

"I **can't** ever have enough!" Aaron replied, who was known to eat six bowls of cornflakes in one sitting.

"Yes, you can. Anyway, **it's** time to go to school. **You'd** better get a move on or **I'm** going to be late for work." Mum strode out of the kitchen impatiently, her shoes clicking on the floor tiles.

I **mustn't** answer back, Aaron thought. **I'd** only get in trouble.

Then his tummy growled so loudly it sounded like a kettle boiling. Aaron dashed to the pantry and grabbed two handfuls of rice bubbles. "**I'll** have to eat them dry," he mumbled as he ran after his mum, leaving a trail on the floor.

You practise

Choose the correct word to replace each contraction.
Shade ONE bubble in each question.

1 **Which word or words could be replaced with we'd?**

- ⬭ weed
- ⬭ we have
- ⬭ we had
- ⬭ we have had

2 **Which word or words could be replaced with I'll?**

- ⬭ ill
- ⬭ I'm ill
- ⬭ I will
- ⬭ I will not

3 **Which word or words could be replaced with you'll?**

- ⬭ yule
- ⬭ you will
- ⬭ you had
- ⬭ you have

4 **Which word or words could be replaced with you're?**

- ⬭ your
- ⬭ you are
- ⬭ you will
- ⬭ you did

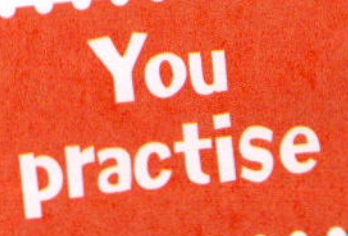

Which sentence uses the apostrophe (') correctly?
Shade ONE bubble in each question.

5
- ⬭ Its time for bed.
- ⬭ It's time for bed.
- ⬭ Its' time for bed.
- ⬭ Its time for'bed.

6
- ⬭ Belle can't take the dogs out today.
- ⬭ Belle cant' take the dogs out today.
- ⬭ Belle cant take the dogs out today.
- ⬭ Belle cant take the dogs' out today.

7
- ⬭ You've got to make your mind up soon.
- ⬭ You'd got to make your mind up soon.
- ⬭ You got to make your mind up soon.
- ⬭ You'll got to make your mind up soon.

8
- ⬭ Theyre running late again.
- ⬭ Their running late again.
- ⬭ There running late again.
- ⬭ They're running late again.

BOB time!

APOSTROPHES for POSSESSION

Possession, or ownership, means something belongs to a person or thing. In sentences, the person or thing is a noun (e.g. *girl*), proper noun (e.g. *Jane*) or pronoun (e.g. *you*).

Possession is shown by using an apostrophe ' and adding the letter 's' at the end of the noun.
The apostrophe comes **between** the noun and the 's'.

Jane's cat	The cat belongs to Jane.
The cat's toys	The toys belong to the cat.

If a plural doesn't end in 's', add an 's' and put the apostrophe **before** it
e.g. *the women's toilets*.

Avoid this common trap:
Don't confuse plurals with possession.
This mistake is often made on signs. For example *Open Sunday's* and *Taxi's* are both wrong – there should be no apostrophes in these words.

Where does the missing apostrophe (') go? Shade ONE bubble in each question.

The boy ● s ○ computer shut down suddenly.

The boy ○ s ● bedrooms were very messy.

It was Thoma ○ s ● decision.

It was the people ● s ○ decision.

We practise

You practise

Where does the missing apostrophe (') go?
Shade ONE bubble in each question.

1. The toy ○○ s battery need ○○ s to be replaced.

2. The dog ○○ s ran across the farmer ○○ s field.

3. The ladie ○○ s toilet ○○ s are closed for cleaning.

4. I read about the election ○○ s in Saturday ○○ s paper.

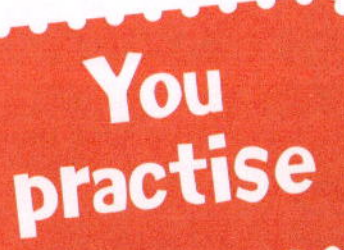

Which sentence uses the apostrophe (') correctly?
Shade ONE bubble in each question.

5.
- ○ I found my mothers' lost earring's.
- ○ I found my mother's lost earring's.
- ○ I found my mother's lost earrings.
- ○ I found my mothers' lost earrings'.

6.
- ○ The mother's group meets once a week.
- ○ The mothers' group meets once a week.
- ○ The mother's group meet's once a week.
- ○ The mothers' group meets' once a week.

7.
- ○ The raindrop's fell on the car's roof.
- ○ The raindrops' fell on the cars roof.
- ○ The raindrops fell on the car's roof.
- ○ The raindrops fell on the cars' roof.

BOB time!

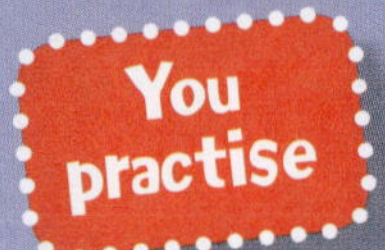

PUNCTUATION TEST 1

Do this test after completing Unit 20. Spend no more than 6 minutes on this test.

Shade ONE bubble for each question to show your answer.

1 Which sentence uses capital letters correctly?

- ⬭ My dog's name is sam. He is two years old.
- ⬭ My dog's name is Sam. He is two years old.
- ⬭ My Dog's name is sam. He is two years old.
- ⬭ My Dog's name is Sam. he is two years old.

2 Where does the missing full stop (.) go?

This jumper was made by ⬭ Aunt ⬭ Sue ⬭ It ⬭ is very warm.

3 Where does the missing comma (,) go?

George's favourite ⬭ lunch ⬭ is lamb ⬭ potatoes ⬭ and peas.

4 Where does the missing comma (,) go?

Because ⬭ you asked ⬭ so nicely ⬭ you may ⬭ have an ice cream.

5 Which sentence has the correct punctuation?

- ⬭ "It's nearly home time" Mr Jennings said.
- ⬭ "It's nearly home time Mr Jennings said".
- ⬭ "It's nearly home time", Mr Jennings said.
- ⬭ "It's nearly home time," Mr Jennings said.

6 Which sentence has the correct punctuation?

- ⬭ "Are you coming to my party," Belinda asked.
- ⬭ "Are you coming to my party?" Belinda asked.
- ⬭ "Are you coming to my party"? Belinda asked
- ⬭ "Are you coming to my party", Belinda asked.

7 Which one of the following should end with a question mark?

- ⬭ I asked you what your name is
- ⬭ What is your name
- ⬭ Your name is John
- ⬭ I think your name is John

BOB time!

PUNCTUATION TEST 2

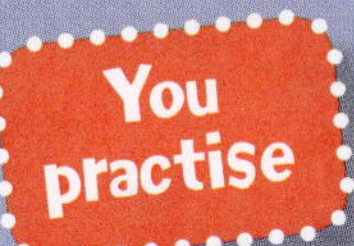

Do this test after completing Unit 24. Spend no more than 6 minutes on this test.

Shade ONE bubble for each question to show your answer.

1 Which punctuation symbol completes the sentence correctly?

Julia walked out, then re entered the room.

- ○ - (hyphen)
- ○ – (dash)

2 Which punctuation symbol completes the sentence correctly?

I thought it was going to rain   but it started to snow.

- ○ - (hyphen)
- ○ – (dash)

3 Which sentence has the correct punctuation?

- ○ The river is overflowing: it has been raining for many days.
- ○ The river is overflowing it has been: raining for many days.
- ○ The river is overflowing; it has been raining for many days.
- ○ The river is overflowing it has been; raining for many days.

4 Which sentence has the correct punctuation?

- ○ We need to buy some: colourful streamers red, green and blue.
- ○ We need to buy some colourful streamers: red, green and blue.
- ○ We need to buy some; colourful streamers red, green and blue.
- ○ We need to buy some colourful streamers; red, green and blue.

5 Where does the missing apostrophe (') go?

Kosta does ○ n ○ t believe that ghost ○ s ○ are real.

6 Where does the missing apostrophe (') go?

It ○ s ○ not surprising the dog lost it ○ s ○ ball.

7 Which sentence uses the apostrophe (') correctly?

- ○ Chris little brother plays with toy cars'.
- ○ Chris' little brother plays with toy cars.
- ○ Chris's little brother plays with toy cars.
- ○ Chris little brother plays with toy car's.

8 Which sentence uses the apostrophe (') correctly?

- ○ Thomas' aunty had twin baby girl's.
- ○ Thomas' aunty had twin baby girls.
- ○ Thomas aunty had twin baby girls'.

BOB time!

ANSWERS

Pre-test

1 impossible
2 happiest
3 training
4 witches
5 leaves
6 The man with black boots entered the damp, dark cave.
7 Leon has been learning the piano since he was four years old.
8 across
9 running
10 play
11 The gardener hummed a tune while mowing the lawn.
12 Fiona, Zayn and Liam want to be in a rock band when they grow up.
13 "Can you hear me now?" Rick asked.
14 Come and meet my co-workers: Ali, David and Emma.
15 It's time you gave the dog its lunch.

Unit 1

1 impossible
2 disadvantage
3 illogical
4 informal
5 misunderstood
6 inconsistent
7 displease
8 immortal
9 irreplaceable
10 reappeared

Unit 2

1 interesting
2 suntanned
3 quaking
4 ugliest
5 hopeful
6 jumping
7 funniest
8 beautiful
9 sheepish
10 expensive

Unit 3

1 sore
2 mousse
3 mail
4 their
5 through
6 lead (homograph)
7 trip (homonym)
8 right (homonym)
9 wind (homograph)
10 minute (homograph)

Unit 4

1 receive
2 floated
3 quiz
4 leaf
5 clouds
6 field
7 queen
8 beans
9 nails
10 should

Unit 5

1 neck
2 badge
3 socks
4 backpack
5 watch
6 fetch
7 edge
8 tragic
9 engaged
10 witch

Unit 6

1 tomatoes
2 leeches
3 sheep
4 classes
5 dishes
6 beaches
7 taxes
8 kangaroos
9 viruses
10 hairbrushes

Unit 7

1 loaves
2 bellies
3 lice
4 academies
5 chefs
6 puffs
7 supplies
8 leaves
9 enemies
10 jeans

Unit 8

1 indices
2 fungi
3 analyses
4 larvae
5 radii
6 cacti
7 bacteria
8 appendices
9 phenomena
10 algae

Spelling test 1

1 illegal
2 baking
3 disappearance
4 bawled
5 ceiling
6 immortal
7 dizziest
8 unreliable
9 knead
10 goal

Spelling test 2

1 manic
2 stopwatches
3 advantages
4 churches
5 fungi
6 rich
7 courage
8 babies
9 knives
10 crises

Unit 9

1 Five seagulls fought for the scraps of bread.
2 The long wooden table was covered with a clean, white tablecloth.
3 The long wooden table was covered with a clean, white tablecloth.
4 A couple of singers performed at the school down the road.
5 A couple of singers performed at the school down the road.
6 the frightened cat
7 the man with a walking stick
8 the dogs in the street
9 twelve children

ANSWERS

Unit 10

1 majestic
2 blue
3 threadbare, gritty, dirty
4 damp, dark
5 big and hairy
6 steaming hot
7 sweet, juicy
8 big mysterious
9 with the green eyes

Unit 11

1 I love walking along the beach.
2 Indira hammered in the nail with all her strength.
3 Eat your dinner before you have dessert.
4 Yesterday I hurt my foot.
5 I found the lost library book under my bed.
6 when I was ill
7 because it was Saturday
8 today
9 in the oven

Unit 12

1 over
2 behind ('under' and 'in' are also possible)
3 on
4 under
5 in
6 the
7 a
8 across
9 during
10 under

Unit 13

1 fell
2 coming
3 ride
4 making
5 did
6 bit
7 break
8 brought
9 caught

Unit 14

1 run
2 runs
3 are
4 is
5 sits
6 is
7 are
8 were
9 am
10 are

Unit 15

1 The car would not start because the battery was flat.
2 You cannot enter the swimming carnival unless you can swim.
3 Nelson swept the floor because it was dirty.
4 After we have lunch, we'll go for a walk.
5 Once she has saved enough money, Gina is going overseas.
6 The car would not start because the battery was flat.
7 You cannot enter the swimming carnival unless you can swim.
8 Nelson swept the floor because it was dirty.
9 After we have lunch, we'll go for a walk.
10 Once she has saved enough money, Gina is going overseas.

Unit 16

1 after
2 until
3 while
4 Because
5 if
6 after
7 before
8 Unless
9 so
10 Although

Grammar test 1

1 Dad's car
2 The boy with the blue T-shirt
3 hotter than usual
4 in full school uniform
5 down the stairs
6 next week
7 through
8 under

Grammar test 2

1 broke
2 choose
3 is
4 are
5 although
6 if
7 Chris kept watch while Tom and Jack went to sleep.
8 Whenever she hears music, Carol starts to sing along.

Unit 17

1 Socks, Saturday
2 Pet Paradise
3 Ben, I
4 Cairns, Monday
5 Louise did not go to school today. Her head aches and her throat is sore.
6 Dad went fishing on Sunday. I went with him and we caught a big fish.
7 Yesterday we went to Bondi Beach. We spent the whole day swimming.

Unit 18

1 today,
2 vegetables,
3 am, see,
4 Australian, red,
5 Although frightening, most earthquakes do not cause any damage.
6 The earthquake made my bed, desk and wardrobe tremble.
7 The whole house shook, but luckily nothing was broken.

Unit 19

1 "We ... kitchen,"
2 "How ... us?"
3 "Great ... yes!"
4 "Maybe ... tomorrow."
5 "Is this the correct answer?" Mia asked.
6 "Careful, you nearly hit me in the head with that ball!" Matthew shouted.
7 The teacher asked, "Did you remember to do your homework?"
8 "I know what you mean," Simon said. "I agree with you!"

ANSWERS

Unit 20

1 something?"
2 socks?"
3 now!"
4 you!
5 "What time does school finish on sports days?" Shirley asked.
6 Shirley wondered what time school finishes on sports days.
7 It is my birthday tomorrow and I can't wait to see my presents!

Unit 21

1 My big brother is getting married, so soon I will have a sister-in-law.
2 Mum says her co-workers are very nice.
3 My brothers – Cody, Sam and Harry – are all taller than me.
4 Re-creation of the crime can help solve who did it.
5 I thought I knew the answer – but clearly I was wrong.
6 long-term
7 re-buffed
8 "I wish you would – oh never mind," Rory muttered.
9 I need three things – lettuce, tomato and cucumber – to make a salad.

Unit 22

1 : (colon)
2 ; (semicolon)
3 : (colon)
4 : (colon)
5 ; (semicolon)
6 For dinner last night we had: roast beef, potatoes and peas.
7 It was zero degrees outside; Brian was worried he might get frostbite.
8 Dingo: a wild dog of Australia, having a reddish-brown or tan coat.

Unit 23

1 we had
2 I will
3 you will
4 you are
5 It's time for bed.
6 Belle can't take the dogs out today.
7 You've got to make your mind up soon.
8 They're running late again.

Unit 24

1 toy's
2 farmer's
3 ladies'
4 Saturday's
5 I found my mother's lost earrings.
6 The mothers' group meets once a week.
7 The raindrops fell on the car's roof.

Punctuation test 1

1 My dog's name is Sam. He is two years old.
2 This jumper was made by Aunt Sue. It is very warm.
3 George's favourite lunch is lamb, potatoes and peas.
4 Because you asked so nicely, you may have an ice cream.
5 "It's nearly home time," Mr Jennings said.
6 "Are you coming to my party?" Belinda asked.
7 What is your name?

Punctuation test 2

1 - (hyphen)
2 – (dash)
3 The river is overflowing; it has been raining for many days.
4 We need to buy some colourful streamers: red, green and blue.
5 doesn't
6 It's not surprising ...
7 Chris' little brother plays with toy cars.
8 Thomas' aunty had twin baby girls.

Sample NAPLAN test

1 received
2 hedge
3 watch
4 beautiful
5 pair
6 stories
7 written
8 disrespect
9 fungi
10 illegal
11 potatoes
12 torches
13 their
14 fetch
15 float
16 thief
17 children
18 seat
19 driven
20 an
21 panting, red-faced
22 on
23 Although
24 flew
25 the
26 when
27 while
28 beating
29 are
30 We have a new dog called Bentley. He likes to chase balls in the park.
31 "Can I go to Lisa's house?" Julia asked.
32 red,
33 they are
34 truth – or
35 What is your favourite flavour?
36 need:
37 I will give Helen's brother some toys for Christmas.
38 Let's go to Chris' house tomorrow.
39 "I am so hungry!" Ming shouted.
40 Jones'